AF521732

LANDOLL
Ashland, Ohio 44805

DAVID AND THE VERY SCARY GIANT

by Sunny Griffin

Illustrated by Donna Lee Hill

DID YOU KNOW...

David lived long ago when wars were fought with swords and shields?

DID YOU KNOW...

In the army of the Philistines was a giant named Goliath who caused a lot of trouble?

DID YOU KNOW...

David's brothers joined the Israelite army to protect their country from the Philistines?

DID YOU KNOW...

David was too young to be a soldier, so he took care of his father's sheep?

DID YOU KNOW...

David's good friends were the lambs he cared for each day and protected from wild animals at night?

DID YOU KNOW...

In the fields with the sheep, David played his harp and sang songs praising God?

DID YOU KNOW...

David loved and trusted God with all his heart?

DID YOU KNOW...

One day, David's father sent him to the Israelite campsite with food for his brothers?

DID YOU KNOW...

Across the valley, David saw Goliath, yelling and boasting that all the Israelites were afraid of him?

DID YOU KNOW...

David was not afraid of Goliath because David trusted God?

DID YOU KNOW...

David put five small, smooth stones in his bag and stepped forward to face Goliath?

DID YOU KNOW...

With his slingshot, David threw a stone that hit Goliath in the forehead and killed him?

The Israelites won the battle against the Philistines because of David's great faith and trust in God.